THE JOURNEY TO SIGNIFICANCE

BREAKING

THE GRIP OF

FEAR

Living A Fear-Free Life

Matthew
Ashimolowo

© 2002 Matthew Ashimolowo

Published by Mattyson Media an imprint of
MAMM
Matthew Ashimolowo Media Ministries
57 Waterden Road
Hackney Wick
London
E15 2EE

ISBN 1 874 646 55 4

Bible quotes are from the King James version
Bible unless otherwise stated.

INTRODUCTION

One of the spirits ruling our society is the spirit of fear. It is as if our world has been put under arrest. This has been so because of the fear of disease, as we read of rising statistical data of HIV, Aids, cancer and other incurable diseases. Furthermore we hear global reports of accidents, wars and rumours of wars.

Earthquakes, disasters and catastrophes taking place in various corners of the earth as well as television and newspapers have not helped either. While they have helped in the process of making our world a global village, yet the news they bring causes fear and consternation and releases upon people what makes them come under a kind of bondage.

There is an upsurge in certain parts of the world of hired assassins; violent crimes are taking place everyday.

Business partners disagreeing and therefore sending hired killers to exterminate their partners. The betrayal of friends and associates, sibling rivalry; all these have increased the chances of fear ruling upon people.

The sociological and political instabilities in many societies have also aggravated the situation. There is an increase in criminal activity all over the world. It certainly is a challenging time to live. At such times the believer must recognise what fear is and that it is a controlling spirit that wants to destroy him.

The spirit of fear is opposed to your destination and wants to stop you from getting there. Fear is the nature of the kingdom of satan, that is why God said He did not give it to you. If you have it, it did not come from your Father. It is not coming from God therefore we can renounce it, reject it, release ourselves from it and let it go from you.

> For God hath not given us the spirit of fear; but of
> power, and of love, and of a sound mind.
> 2 Timothy 1:7 (KJV)

The Scripture says in 1 Corinthians 3:21, "All things are yours." But that does not include satan's property. Fear is the nature of the devil and therefore it cannot have come from the Father. It is an ugly thing that manifests itself from many directions. It is a seed that can be sown into our hearts from childhood so that a person can grow into adulthood but be controlled all their life by the spirit of fear.

And, ye fathers, provoke not your children to wrath: but
bring them up in the nurture and admonition of the
Lord.
Ephesians 6:4 (KJV)

Satan requires fear to operate his kingdom because
through it he can hand you a bill of goods that is not
yours. Unless you know how to be bold and reject what
he hands to you, it can become complicated because along
with what he hands over to you he brings other things. So
when satan tries to pass on properties that are not yours,
the best thing is to let him know that you do not want
them.

Fear is a weak spirit that comes from the bottomless pit of
hell. It is something you must refuse before it gains
ground. It is something you must break before it begins
to manifest from your heart through all of your life.

There are different kinds of fears but the Lord wants to
deliver you from them all.

I sought the LORD, and he heard me, and delivered me
from all my fears.
Psalms 34:4 (KJV)

Psychologists tell us that 85% of the things we are afraid
of never happen. People suffer from all kinds of fear,
phobias and anxieties. People suffer from the fear of flying,
fear of heights, fear of the dark, fear of crossing bridges,
fear of going through tunnels. Fear certainly has no
respect of persons. The world does not consider any news

to be worth sharing unless it is bad news that causes fear. As a result everything around the world seems to be pro-grammed around fear.

Fear grips people; it disturbs their way of thinking and makes a big thing out of small things. Fear is a magnifier of problems; it is an instrument of intimidation from the devil. It is one of his best tactics and methods for limiting people and holding them in a pattern of failure.

It is the apprehension of evil. When people walk in fear they lack courage. They panic at the sight of the smallest of problems and become very cowardly. They lose nerve in the face of a battle or run away from any responsibility that is challenging.

Fear is the opposite of faith.

What shall we then say to these things? If God be for us, who can be against us?
Romans 8:31 (KJV)

Be not afraid of their faces: for I am with thee to deliver thee, saith the LORD.
Jeremiah 1:8 (KJV)

Fear itself is a sickness or disease; a spirit that binds and takes away joy.

Ye are of God, little children, and have overcome them: because greater is he that is in you, than he that is in the world.
1 John 4:4 (KJV)

The irony of fear is that what you are afraid of is more likely to happen because you have walked in fear.

For the thing which I greatly feared is come upon me,
and that which I was afraid of is come unto me.
Job 3:25 (KJV)

It torments people and it is one of satan's best weapons.

DiFfErent KinDs of FEars

F

ear is: apprehension, consternation, dismay, disquiet, dread, fright, horror, misgiving, panic, terror, timidity, trembling, tremor, and trepidation.

It may be sudden or lingering in view of present or imminent danger. Fear is sometimes horrific, particularly when it is accompanied by something abhorrent. Fear could be a sudden encounter when someone sees a ghastly spectacle.

Another word for fear is timidity. Timidity is a quality or habit or condition or a readiness to be affected with fear. Timid people are constantly liable to fear even when there is no cause for alarm.

There is:

Acrophobia - fear of heights
Agoraphobia - fear of open spaces
Ailurophoia - fear of cats
Agliophobia - fear of pain
Androphobia - fear of men
Astraphobia - fear of thunder and lightening
Autophobia - fear of being alone
Bathophobia - fear of depth
Claustrophobia - fear of closed space
Cynophobia - fear of dogs
Demophobia - fear of crowds
Dromophobia - fear of crossing streets
Genophobia - fear of sex
Gynophobia - fear of women
Haptephobia - fear of touch
Hemophobia - fear of blood
Hydrophobia - fear of water
Hypnophobia - fear of falling asleep
Misophobia - fear of contamination
Musophobia - fear of mice
Neophobia - fear of the new
Noctiphobia - fear of the night or darkness
Ophidiophobia - fear of snakes
Photophobia - fear of light
Sitophobia - fear of food or eating
Taphephobia - fear of being buried alive
Thantophobia - fear of death
Toxicophobia - fear of poison
Xenophobia - fear of foreigners
Zoophobia - fear of animals

In addition some others are:

Fear of flying - Aviophobia
Fear of thunder - Ceraunophobia
Fear of old age - Gerontophobia
Fear of poverty or lack - Peniaphobia
Fear of rejection
Fear of the future

Sometimes people would use information they have about you or concerning you to try to put you in fear. People are sometimes afraid of sickness and disease.

> And he answered, Fear not: for they that be with us are
> more than they that be with them.
> 2 Kings 6:16 (KJV)

Yet in spite of all these descriptions, our strength in the Lord must be increased until we are not bound by fear.

> Finally, my brethren, be strong in the Lord, and in the
> power of his might.
> Ephesians 6:10 (KJV)

WHY YOU MUST BREAK THE BACKBONE OF FEAR?

Little does one realise that from upbringing, seeds of fear are often planted by the method of those who brought us up. The abuse of parents or friends, brothers, cousins or uncles can leave an indelible mark and expose the victim to perpetual phobia.

1. You need to break the backbone of fear because you need to make an impact

To achieve anything substantial, you must once in a while go against the flow, in spite of how your heart wants to make you timid. Those who are fearful and afraid never confront their enemy and overcome them.

> Now therefore go to, proclaim in the ears of the people, saying, Whosoever is fearful and afraid, let him return and depart early from mount Gilead. And there returned of the people twenty and two thousand; and there remained ten thousand.
> Judges 7:3 (KJV)

The irony about fear is that it feeds on your anxiety and on the atmosphere of strife. So you must break its backbone or else every anxiety and every challenge you face, every turmoil, every confusion gives the fear you face more weight.

> For thus saith the Lord GOD, the Holy One of Israel; In returning and rest shall ye be saved; in quietness and in confidence shall be your strength: and ye would not.
> Isaiah 30:15 (KJV)

2. You must break the backbone of fear because satan would take advantage of it and use it to control you

Fear is satan's nature which he gave to you. It makes you to agree to satanic symptoms instead of rebelling against them. It makes you to accept certain battles as inevitable. Fear is a nature that belongs to your old life, it is of satan. You must break its backbone because you now belong in the kingdom of light.

3. You must break the backbone of fear because God promises to be your exceeding great reward

This means that He will protect you and be there for you and therefore you have no reason to be afraid of the future.

> After these things the word of the LORD came unto Abram in a vision, saying, Fear not, Abram: I am thy shield, and thy exceeding great reward.
> Genesis 15:1 (KJV)

4. You must break the backbone of fear because one of its methods is to give the impression that you are exposed and unprotected

That contradicts God's Word.

> God is our refuge and strength, a very present help in trouble. Therefore will not we fear, though the earth be removed, and though the mountains be carried into the midst of the sea; Though the waters thereof roar and be troubled, though the mountains shake with the swelling thereof. Selah.
> Psalms 46:1-3 (KJV)

5. You need to know you can break the backbone of fear because God promises to stand by you

Fear thou not; for I am with thee: be not dismayed; for
I am thy God: I will strengthen thee; yea, I will help
thee; yea, I will uphold thee with the right hand of my
righteousness.
Isaiah 41:10 (KJV)

For I the LORD thy God will hold thy right hand,
saying unto thee, Fear not; I will help thee. Fear not,
thou worm Jacob, and ye men of Israel; I will help thee,
saith the LORD, and thy redeemer, the Holy One of
Israel. Behold, I will make thee a new sharp threshing
instrument having teeth: thou shalt thresh the
mountains, and beat them small, and shalt make the
hills as chaff.
Isaiah 41:13-15 (KJV)

The confidence of the believer should rise with the knowledge that he is not alone. The God of the Universe has
chosen to stand with him.

6. You should break the backbone of fear because we have the promise of God in moments of challenges to deliver us out of whatever trouble we find ourselves

And Moses said unto the people, Fear ye not, stand still,
and see the salvation of the LORD, which he will shew
to you to day: for the Egyptians whom ye have

seen to day, ye shall see them again no more for ever.
The LORD shall fight for you, and ye shall hold your
peace.
Exodus 14:13-14 (KJV)

7. You should not be afraid because you already have the victory before the battle began

That should be enough confidence for the believer that there is nothing to be afraid of.

And the LORD said unto Joshua, Fear not, neither be
thou dismayed: take all the people of war with thee, and
arise, go up to Ai: see, I have given into thy hand the
king of Ai, and his people, and his city, and his land:
Joshua 8:1 (KJV)

Nay, in all these things we are more than conquerors
through him that loved us.
Romans 8:37 (KJV)

We need to express confidence and boldness and break the backbone of fear:

8. Because if we are afraid in the face of every challenge, how do we expect to run the kingdom of God if we are unable to cope with the smallest of challenges?

But rather seek ye the kingdom of God; and all these
things shall be added unto you. Fear not, little flock;

for it is your Father's good pleasure to give you the
kingdom.
Luke 12:31-32 (KJV)

For ye have not received the spirit of bondage again to
fear; but ye have received the Spirit of adoption,
whereby we cry, Abba, Father.
Romans 8:15 (KJV)

You are a poor specimen if you can't stand the pressure
of adversity.
Proverbs 24:10 (Living)

9.   You must break the backbone of fear because it is your heritage to operate in boldness and not fear

The wicked flee when no man pursueth: but the
righteous are bold as a lion.
Proverbs 28:1 (KJV)

10.   You should not be afraid because the battle really is not yours, it belongs to God and if it is His, He will see you through

Ye shall not need to fight in this battle: set yourselves,
stand ye still, and see the salvation of the LORD with
you, O Judah and Jerusalem: fear not, nor be dismayed;
to morrow go out against them: for the LORD will be
with you.
2 Chronicles 20:17 (KJV)

Fear is a bad thing which becomes a stopper. It served the enemy in belittling and limiting Israel from entering and maximising her promised land. It has the ability to keep a person from entering the fullness of the provision Christ has for him. Just as it kept Israel from all that it had on the other side of Jordan, fear can stop you from moving into the fullness of God's calling on your life and the maximisation of your ministry.

Fear can hold you in sickness and disease and justify the position in which you have found yourself. Fear has a nagging way of justifying poverty, lack and conditions that are not conducive or in agreement with the finished work of Jesus Christ on the cross.

HOW

FEAR

COMES

I had the unpleasant experience of having to break the news of the death of the father of one of my staff. Having a young family, the lady had to come with her husband and her daughter; we wanted it to be in an unsuspecting way because she was pregnant. On breaking the news she broke down in tears in front of her three year-old. From that day on, whenever they suggested coming to visit my house, the image the three year-old has had of my house is that it was where her mother was made to cry uncontrollably. It has instilled some kind of fear in the little child.

Trauma, accidents, incidences that are shocking, these have often been inroads for fear. People's actions and reactions around us can also set us in motion to walk and express unnecessary phobias. A spouse in an abusive relationship, a friend with a controlling partner, people working in places of employment where they are given the impression of continuous uncertainty live perpetually under the 'Sword of Damocles' of the spirit of fear.

Fear can make a person withdraw into a dream world or revert to violent and defensive attitudes. It is my opinion that fear for a child at the sight of images, impressions and emotional challenges it cannot handle can result in an almost permanent emotional damage.

For example if a child from two or three persistently observes violent behaviour from parents, the child in my opinion can withdraw into a cocoon. It can affect the child's capacity to express himself and we may safely conclude that it is a reason for autism.

1. **Fear comes when people receive bad news**

2. **Fear comes when people use threatening words**

3. **Fear can follow when businesses go into a downward spiral and we begin to imagine every evil that can happen to us**

4. **Fear comes when people hear bad news and also meditate on it**

Fear is a product of sin and rebellion against God.

And he said, I heard thy voice in the garden, and I was afraid, because I was naked; and I hid myself.
Genesis 3:10 (KJV)

If thou doest well, shalt thou not be accepted? and if thou doest not well, sin lieth at the door. And unto thee shall be his desire, and thou shalt rule over him.
Genesis 4:7 (KJV)

5. Fear could be the product of a seed of trouble fed by your own imagination ...

...watered by a timid attitude and that has grown to become the unseen monster reaching into your future. It is a spirit sent from hell to destroy; once it is entertained it makes its room until it invites other spirits like the spirit of death and hell.

6. The entrance of fear is obviously through words

And Isaiah said unto them, Thus shall ye say unto your master, Thus saith the LORD, Be not afraid of the words that thou hast heard, wherewith the servants of the king of Assyria have blasphemed me. Behold, I will send a blast upon him, and he shall hear a rumour, and return to his own land; and I will cause him to fall by the sword in his own land.
Isaiah 37:6-7 (KJV)

Be not afraid of their faces: for I am with thee to deliver thee, saith the LORD.
Jeremiah 1:8 (KJV)

And Moses said unto the people, Fear ye not, stand still, and see the salvation of the LORD, which he will shew to you to day: for the Egyptians whom ye have seen

to day, ye shall see them again no more for ever.
Exodus 14:13 (KJV)

Thou shalt not be afraid for the terror by night; nor for
the arrow that flieth by day;
Psalms 91:5 (KJV)

When thou goest out to battle against thine enemies,
and seest horses, and chariots, and a people more than
thou, be not afraid of them: for the LORD thy God is
with thee, which brought thee up out of the land of
Egypt. And shall say unto them, Hear, O Israel, ye
approach this day unto battle against your enemies: let
not your hearts faint, fear not, and do not tremble,
neither be ye terrified because of them;
Deuteronomy 20:1,3 (KJV)

And he said, Hearken ye, all Judah, and ye inhabitants
of Jerusalem, and thou king Jehoshaphat, Thus saith
the LORD unto you, Be not afraid nor dismayed by
reason of this great multitude; for the battle is not yours,
but God's.
2 Chronicles 20:15 (KJV)

From the scriptures quoted...

7. ...fear is a product of words, faces of men, terrors
that fly by day and night, the magnitude and power
of the people who rise up against you

Whatever happens fear requires your permission to magnify circumstances, situations, faces and facts to be elevated
above the Word of God.

8. It is a satanic blanket created for his overt and covert operation

Once thrown over you, you almost cannot perceive any-thing of God but the lies of the enemy. It is a spirit, but thank God deliverance is possible in Christ Jesus. Fear was allowed to be magnified in the days of the children of Israel until it grew so big and scared them out of their destiny.

> And Moses said unto the people, Fear ye not, stand still, and see the salvation of the LORD, which he will shew to you to day: for the Egyptians whom ye have seen to day, ye shall see them again no more for ever.
> Exodus 14:13 (KJV)

We see Moses responding and letting the people know that the only thing that can stop them and keep them on this side of the Red Sea was fear itself. Fear comes when you strive in the flesh for things that are of little value in the kingdom of God. Fear operates on the seed-bed of the power of suggestion. When satan begins to suggest the consequences of what you are going through, you imme-diately are unable to see how God makes a way where there seems to be no way.

All the promises given you, the assurances spoken in your heart seem to jump out of the window.

THE pOISONOUS POWER OF fEAR

Fear does destroy, causing intense trouble to those whom its fangs have gripped. When fear comes it opens the door to all kinds of troubles, sickness, diseases etc.

A merry heart maketh a cheerful countenance: but by
sorrow of the heart the spirit is broken.
Proverbs 15:13 (KJV)

A merry heart doeth good like a medicine: but a broken
spirit drieth the bones.
Proverbs 17:22 (KJV)

Every negative reaction is said to produce toxins which poison the blood vessels, tissue and the general body system. It is said that there is a link between cancerous cells, heart trouble and a fearful heart. In effect fear brings people into all kinds of bondage.

The fear of man bringeth a snare: but whoso putteth his trust in the LORD shall be safe.

Proverbs 29:25 (KJV)

For the thing which I greatly feared is come upon me, and that which I was afraid of is come unto me.

Job 3:25 (KJV)

When you bring yourself into a state of fear of men, employees, employers, husbands, wives, you lose everything God has for you.

The reason this happens is that,

1. Fear releases pressure

And where there is pressure, joy becomes drained, health, victory and every positive aspect of your life is ruined. What follows is defeat, sadness and failure, where one's life should have known victory.

2. Fear makes you dote on your shortcomings

The man who walks in fear never draws from the strength, the positive things in his life. A fearful heart produces grumbling, complaining and a bitter spirit, and where bitterness is the Holy Spirit cannot be found to thrive. We all have found ourselves in circumstances where the natural reaction is fear. Finances are not going well, family issues, you are left with mountains of indebtedness and you do not know what to do. We are told for example of the woman whose husband left her with indebtedness and

8. Fear can open the gate of hell, the door of death and expose you to sudden danger

The fear of man can become a trap that holds you where you do not belong or fit.

> The fear of man bringeth a snare: but whoso putteth his trust in the LORD shall be safe.
> Proverbs 29:25 (KJV)

> For God hath not given us the spirit of fear; but of power, and of love, and of a sound mind.
> 2 Timothy 1:7 (KJV)

9. The first aim of fear is to destroy you; it does this by trying to bind you, torment you and hold you perpetually in terror or dread

Fear makes you have a constant expectation of evil or trouble; a belief that thing will always go wrong.

10. Fear causes you to expect the worse; fear can put you in bondage to the thing you were afraid of

At such times one of the cheapest ways to break the power of satan and sin is to expose the thing with which he wants to condemn you.

11. Fear can make you shy and cause you to have a timid attitude

Fear can stop you from witnessing so you stay silent

because you feel you are likely to be embarrassed to share your faith.

It is not only satan who uses fear; people will try to intimidate or take advantage of you because of reports, opportunities they have or information that has come to light and they have by privilege.

12. Fear results in bondage, and bondage is always the result of satan's work

Fear is a little thing that can become a big one. Small fears if not checked become big ones, big fears if not checked become a major bondage and a major bondage unchecked becomes a doorway for the devil.

13. Fear undermines your enthusiasm for life

It takes advantage of a predicament you have found yourself in and tries to use it to control you.

And now I exhort you to be of good cheer: for there shall
be no loss of any man's life among you, but of
the ship.
Acts 27:22 (KJV)

14. Fear quenches and discourages initiative

It takes away the step of faith so that everything you are doing is either in the flesh or based on natural knowledge. When a person or organisation is bound by fear, it leads to uncertainty of purpose, it will discourage and hold back initiative, innovation and the ability to carry out projects for fear that they might fail.

15. Fear encourages procrastination and mediocrity so that you are full of activity without progress

Fear kills love, the Bible says, "There is no fear in love..."

There is no fear in love; but perfect love casteth out fear: because fear hath torment. He that feareth is not made perfect in love.
1 John 4:18 (KJV)

16. It breeds jealousy and suspicion. Fear produces the feeling of rejection

Fear diverts your concentration and breaks your focus, so that instead of focusing on the Lord you focus on the circumstance.

But when he saw the wind boisterous, he was afraid; and beginning to sink, he cried, saying, Lord, save me.
Matthew 14:30 (KJV)

17. Fear is a paralysing force that is making all effort to severely handicap your calling and your potential for success

18. Fear builds invisible walls and erects barriers between people, therefore destroying human relationships

It feeds our imagination and makes us suspect people who would have been a blessing to us.

19. Every form of racial prejudice is fed by fear

Particularly the fear of the unknown and where we do not know enough about people, our imagination runs wild.

20. Fear can pull you away from serving God

So that you say, "I'm not good enough, I'm not holy enough, I'm not useful enough, I'm not eloquent enough, I'm not old enough."

21. Fear can prevent you from witnessing and telling others about Jesus, so you stay silent instead of sharing the good news of Jesus Christ

Then they said one to another, We do not well: this day is a day of good tidings, and we hold our peace: if we tarry till the morning light, some mischief will come upon us: now therefore come, that we may go and tell the king's household.
2 Kings 7:9 (KJV)

Fear can make you an unfruitful, ineffective minister of the kingdom. When fear steps in you are likely to think and act irrationally and this will result in panic decisions, knee jerk reactions.

22. **Fear is designed to hold you back and contain you so that it prevents you from going forward or maximising your life**

23. **Severe fear can deny you good health, good sleep, so that instead of meditating on the Word of the Lord your mind is on the situation**

God's promise is only to keep in peace those whose mind is stayed on him.

> Thou wilt keep him in perfect peace, whose mind is
> stayed on thee: because he trusteth in thee.
> Isaiah 26:3 (KJV)

24. **Fear destroys your capacity to rest and ultimately results in your loss of mind sometimes**

People who are acutely depressed or have moved into paranoia or schizophrenia have been known to start with certain fears.

25. **Fear can choke your spiritual growth, hinder it and prevent you from fulfilling the will of God for your life**

How many men and women may be reading this book who have been called to ministry but for fear of failure or the thought that to be in ministry is an economic risk may have never taken the step?

Fear can cause containment so that instead of you coming into the fullness of your purpose in life, you are contained within one place.

fREEDOM

FROM

FEAR

A man will boast of how he will fare in battle until the battle really rages. From all we have shared it is obvious that fear is a weapon of satan. Knowing well that through external encirclement he cannot hit as much, satan specialises in using internal demoralisation.

Internal demoralisation begins with an attack by the spirit of fear. It is fed furthermore by how close or distant we are from daily meditation in the Word of God. It is the entrance of God's Word that makes the path of the righteous to shine. It is the entrance of God's Word that makes the righteous to be as bold as a lion. Without a constant supply of God's Word we begin to live on suggestions and we are carried away by the things we see, hear or feel and not led by the Lord.

For as many as are led by the Spirit of God, they are the
sons of God.
Romans 8:14 (KJV)

We know we can be free from fear because God promises
to be the One to whom we can "steal away."

God is our refuge and strength, a very present help in
trouble. Therefore will not we fear, though the earth be
removed, and though the mountains be carried into the
midst of the sea;
Psalms 46:1-2 (KJV)

So when God becomes our refuge and our strength, what
trouble can scare the believer's heart? Trust becomes a
strong element in breaking the power of fear. We just
have to trust God during those silent moments when
solutions have not been found to the challenges we face.
When answers have not come forth to the questions we
have, that God will still make good the promises He has
made.

What time I am afraid, I will trust in thee. In God I
will praise his word, in God I have put my trust; I will
not fear what flesh can do unto me... When I cry unto
thee, then shall mine enemies turn back: this I know; for
God is for me.
Psalms 56:3-4,9 (KJV)

A trusting heart will cry to God, a trusting heart will
report the matter to God instead of taking the matters in
its own hand.

Ferocious men will boast; the people who think they have information on us will look at us in the face and try to scare us. Those who think they have more on their side than us, who think they have surrounded us and we have no way of escape, will boast and rejoice in what they can do to us, but in the words of David, "The Lord on our side" tilts the balance.

The LORD is on my side; I will not fear: what can man
do unto me?
Psalms 118:6 (KJV)

When all is said and done, the faithfulness of God will become manifest and in His faithfulness He will stabilize, establish, strengthen and put your foot on the ground.

BREAKING

THE

BACKBONE

OF **FEAR**

We have established the fact that when fear is given the backbone, it wants to control, limit, belittle, stop or hinder you from the purpose of God. Yet though fear may have all the manifestations we have mentioned in the previous chapters, yet it can be whipped and overcome. This is the reason Jesus Christ went to the cross of Calvary so that nothing can limit, stop, hold or belittle the potential of the believer.

1. Your walk of victory must start by expressing yourself with thanksgiving and joy

The atmosphere of thanksgiving and joy creates enough anointing to dispel fear and release the boldness of the Lord.

2. The walk of victory must be perpetuated by the application of the Word of God to the situation

When fear knocks and the Word of God opens the door, there will be no one to stand anymore.

> If ye abide in me, and my words abide in you, ye shall ask what ye will, and it shall be done unto you.
> John 15:7 (KJV)

3. You must learn how to manage your ears

The Scriptures call it inclining your ears. If you do not know how to chose, challenge or change how they hear, you will perpetually hear what drains your faith and reduces your confidence. Evil tidings take advantage of your ear gate and cause you to walk in bondage.

> He shall not be afraid of evil tidings: his heart is fixed, trusting in the LORD. His heart is established, he shall not be afraid, until he see his desire upon his enemies.
> Psalms 112:7-8 (KJV)

Before fear makes its maximum impact, begin to gather all the Scriptures that promise you God's victory. The Word of God is your sure instrument in moments of difficulty. Without the Word the chances are that you would allow worry, frustration, fear and confusion to overwhelm you. But the presence of God's Word helps one to have the right godly perspective to the situation.

It gives us an understanding of who God is and what He wants to do in the situation.

> He shall cover thee with his feathers, and under his wings shalt thou trust: his truth shall be thy shield and buckler.
> Psalms 91:4 (KJV)

> A wholesome tongue is a tree of life: but perverseness therein is a breach in the spirit.
> Proverbs 15:4 (KJV)

Proverbs 15:4 talks about the tongue and its part in the process of working in divine victory.

4. The tongue must be used to create victory around you

It must become your tree of life with which you speak life into dead situations; the bridge that carries you from one realm to another. It must become your instrument of your protection, so that instead of saying what the enemy says, with your tongue you make known the report of the Lord.

Your tongue must become the shield against every negative attitude that satan wants you to operate in. At such times discover and focus on the strength of the Lord. Let it be your confidence.

> God is my strength and power: and he maketh my way perfect. He maketh my feet like hinds' feet, and

setteth me upon my high places.
2 Samuel 22:33-34 (KJV)

5. Renounce every satanic deal that has been handed over to you, that does not belong to you

In moments of fear satan has a habit of passing sickness, problems, troubles and makes you call them yours. You must rather choose to renounce it and announce God's Word as your best protection.

Develop an uncommon and a Holy Ghost packed confidence in God, so that irrespective of what you see, it is only the counsel of the Lord that you choose to emphasise.

For thus saith the Lord GOD, the Holy One of Israel; In returning and rest shall ye be saved; in quietness and in confidence shall be your strength: and ye would not.
Isaiah 30:15 (KJV)

And Moses said unto the people, Fear ye not, stand still, and see the salvation of the LORD, which he will shew to you to day: for the Egyptians whom ye have seen to day, ye shall see them again no more for ever. The LORD shall fight for you, and ye shall hold your peace.
Exodus 14:13-14 (KJV)

In God have I put my trust: I will not be afraid what man can do unto me.
Psalms 56:11 (KJV)

In the fear of the LORD is strong confidence: and his
children shall have a place of refuge.
Proverbs 14:26 (KJV)

Because you have defeated fear once does not mean that it
will not strike back. Yet every time it does, your confidence in the Lord must remain constant. That quiet
confident spirit that declares the Word of God in the face
of anxiety, trouble and strife must be your constant stay.

Declaring your trust and expressing confidence in God
releases the anointing, destroys yokes, it removes burdens.
Act as a person who believes God and therefore in antici-
pation of your coming victory begin to lay on the altar of
God the sacrifice of thanksgiving.

It is such faith actions that turn things for the believer.

Save us, O LORD our God, and gather us from among
the heathen, to give thanks unto thy holy name, and to
triumph in thy praise.
Psalms 106:47 (KJV)

And when they began to sing and to praise, the LORD
set ambushments against the children of Ammon, Moab,
and mount Seir, which were come against Judah; and
they were smitten.
2 Chronicles 20:22 (KJV)

And at midnight Paul and Silas prayed, and sang praises
unto God: and the prisoners heard them.
Acts 16:25 (KJV)

Israel's ability to praise God in the face of Jericho's wall, made the wall not to be able to hold for a long time.

6. Victory only comes when you yield to the spirit of victory

It is not a denial of the reality of the battle. It is a choice to magnify the God who is going to turn the battle to a testimony. Did you know that giving God thanksgiving when the worst battle is going on around you is the worst insult you can give to satan?

It smacks him in the face, that irrespective of all his taunts and punches, you give him no regard.

7. Reject and refuse the spirit of condemnation

Remind yourself that if you walk in joy, it releases you from fear. Fear and joy cannot be in the same boat. One has to give way to the other.

Then he said unto them, Go your way, eat the fat, and drink the sweet, and send portions unto them for whom nothing is prepared: for this day is holy unto our Lord: neither be ye sorry; for the joy of the LORD is your strength.
Nehemiah 8:10 (KJV)

Therefore with joy shall ye draw water out of the wells of salvation.
Isaiah 12:3 (KJV)

A merry heart doeth good like a medicine: but a broken
spirit drieth the bones.
Proverbs 17:22 (KJV)

HOW CAN YOU WALK IN JOY?

1. Meditate on all the good things God has done in your life

2. Remember all the blessings He has given you

* A beautiful wife
* A lovely husband
* Godly children
* Bring to your remembrance the financial break-throughs you have enjoyed from God, the open doors, and the favours.
* Take the time to confess the victories that you already hear in your spirit.

3. Maintain an overcomers stand by raising the shield of faith

It is with such action that you are able to stop every fiery
dart of fear and unbelief.

Strengthen ye the weak hands, and confirm the feeble
knees. Say to them that are of a fearful heart, Be strong,
fear not: behold, your God will come with vengeance,
even God with a recompence; he will come and
save you.
Isaiah 35:3-4 (KJV)

And his disciples came to him, and awoke him, saying,
Lord, save us: we perish. And he saith unto them, Why
are ye fearful, O ye of little faith? Then he arose, and
rebuked the winds and the sea; and there was a
great calm.
Matthew 8:25-26 (KJV)

One of the greatest gifts God has given to man is the
power of choice. Make a deliberate choice of faith and
boldness in place of fear and timidity.

Know ye not, that to whom ye yield yourselves servants
to obey, his servants ye are to whom ye obey; whether of
sin unto death, or of obedience unto righteousness?
Romans 6:16 (KJV)

**4. One of satan's chief ways to get you in perpetual
condemnation is if you walk in the atmosphere of sin
and unrighteousness**

Choose holiness, choose to walk right.

I also will choose their delusions, and will bring their
fears upon them; because when I called, none did answer;
when I spake, they did not hear: but they did evil before
mine eyes, and chose that in which I
delighted not.
Isaiah 66:4 (KJV)

But whoso hearkeneth unto me shall dwell safely, and
shall be quiet from fear of evil
Proverbs 1:33 (KJV)

5. Become a God chaser

Let your passion for worship be known. Those who pursue God, who chase after His will, will be surrounded by the boldness of the Lord and the blessing of His presence.

> I sought the LORD, and he heard me, and delivered me
> from all my fears.
> Psalms 34:4 (KJV)

> For he satisfieth the longing soul, and filleth the hungry
> soul with goodness.
> Psalms 107:9 (KJV)

> Fear ye not, neither be afraid: have not I told thee from
> that time, and have declared it? ye are even my
> witnesses. Is there a God beside me? yea, there is no
> God; I know not any.
> Isaiah 44:8 (KJV)

Abide in Christ. If you are found in the Lord always, it becomes a sure way to overcome satan. It is difficult for him to get you, he will have to get God, tear off God and bring out Jesus, tear off Jesus and then bring you out. That is a tall order. Do not step out of Christ; it is your abiding in Him that guarantees perpetual victory.

I cannot forget reading the story of the man who owned an orchard with birds who lived in the orchard. Every time poachers came, they had to attract the birds out of his orchard in order to shoot them because he had built a wall around the orchard. The enemy is constantly trying to distract you out of God's orchard. Stay in your calling, fear will not break you.

Put your faith and righteousness to action.

> Whereby are given unto us exceeding great and precious
> promises: that by these ye might be partakers of the
> divine nature, having escaped the corruption that is in
> the world through lust.
> 2 Peter 1:4 (KJV)

6. Overcome fear by tearing down every stronghold that satan is trying to build

He is using your imagination to lie to you. Do not become a tool in His hands.

> Casting down imaginations, and every high thing that
> exalteth itself against the knowledge of God, and
> bringing into captivity every thought to the obedience
> of Christ;
> 2 Corinthians 10:5 (KJV)

So every time he shoots a contrary thought, bring it to the subjection of Christ. Every time he tells you to walk in fear, remind him that by reason of the finished work of Jesus Christ and your acceptance of Him as your Lord and Saviour, your legal nature is that of love, joy, peace, long-suffering and all other fruit of the Spirit.

When you have done all this remember the instruction of the Lord to Israel in the moments of trouble when they were confronted by the Red Sea. Stand still and see the salvation of the Lord. Stay in the constant remembrance that the reason for the sudden invasion of fear and attack on your mind is because God is about to lift you and take you to another level, while satan is trying to restrict you and hold you in your present mould.

Behold, the LORD thy God hath set the land before thee: go up and possess it, as the LORD God of thy fathers hath said unto thee; fear not, neither be discouraged.
Deuteronomy 1:21 (KJV)

Ye shall not fear them: for the LORD your God he shall fight for you.
Deuteronomy 3:22 (KJV)

The Scripture says that the One who you serve goes before you and He stands behind you. He becomes your covering on every side, so when fear comes, remember the size of the people is not what matters, but the One who is by you to make you win.

Be strong and of a good courage, fear not, nor be afraid of them: for the LORD thy God, he it is that doth go with thee; he will not fail thee, nor forsake thee.
Deuteronomy 31:6 (KJV)

There will be times in your walk when your hand seems weak and your faith does not seem to work. At such times you do not seem to know what to do, but take your courage from God's Word. Encourage yourself. Strengthen yourself in spite of the weakness you see.

> Strengthen ye the weak hands, and confirm the feeble knees. Say to them that are of a fearful heart, Be strong, fear not: behold, your God will come with vengeance, even God with a recompence; he will come and save you.
> Isaiah 35:3-4 (KJV)

We are tempted to always wait for the next word from our pastor. Breaking the backbone of fear may mean you may have to do it yourself sometimes, in the face of apparent defeat and an overwhelming opposing majority. Because sometimes those who rise against you may be more than you, there could be a host of them. Your remembrance should be that they that are for you are more than they that are against you.

> And when the servant of the man of God was risen early, and gone forth, behold, an host compassed the city both with horses and chariots. And his servant said unto him, Alas, my master! how shall we do? And he answered, Fear not: for they that be with us are more than they that be with them.
> 2 Kings 6:15-16 (KJV)

It will require the development of spiritual eyes to be able to see beyond the natural and know that you sometimes seem to be in the minority. You are too precious to God to be left alone. Rest in your position in God. God has snuggled you under His mighty arm. How can you fail when the biggest arms that exist have held you?

The eternal God is thy refuge, and underneath are the everlasting arms: and he shall thrust out the enemy from before thee; and shall say, Destroy them.
Deuteronomy 33:27 (KJV)

7. Develop a disciplined mind

Set your affection on things above, not on things on the earth.
Colossians 3:2 (KJV)

I beseech you therefore, brethren, by the mercies of God, that ye present your bodies a living sacrifice, holy, acceptable unto God, which is your reasonable service.
Romans 12:1 (KJV)

And having done that refuse to be afraid of their faces, of the facts, of your foes - refuse to be afraid of folks that want to stop you.

These actions do not stop fear from continuously barraging your door, but let faith answer and there will be no one there. Be bold, be strong, for the Lord your God is with you. The Lord will be there to fight for you.

Have not I commanded thee? Be strong and of a good courage; be not afraid, neither be thou dismayed: for the LORD thy God is with thee whithersoever thou goest.
Joshua 1:9 (KJV)

Finally, my brethren, be strong in the Lord, and in the
power of his might.
Ephesians 6:10 (KJV)

And he answered, Fear not: for they that be with us are
more than they that be with them.
2 Kings 6:16 (KJV)

When your heart is troubled, remember God is your
refuge and strength.

God is our refuge and strength, a very present help in
trouble. Therefore will not we fear, though the earth be

removed, and though the mountains be carried into the
midst of the sea;
Psalms 46:1-2 (KJV)

When it seems as if He is distant, remember that He will
attend to your prayer.

Hear my cry, O God; attend unto my prayer. From the
end of the earth will I cry unto thee, when my heart is
overwhelmed: lead me to the rock that is higher than I.
Psalms 61:1-2 (KJV)

If it is mercy you need know that He will respond.

But thou, O LORD, be merciful unto me, and raise me
up, that I may requite them.
Psalms 41:10 (KJV)

When you look at the majority of the people against you remember the One who is on your side, and He tilts the balance; you already have a majority of one great God.

The LORD is on my side; I will not fear: what can man do unto me?
Psalms 118:6 (KJV)

CONCLUSION

We have seen the devastating effect of fear, how it has held many in bondage.

* Fear has destroyed kingdoms.
* Fear has made people lose their destiny, their purpose, their blessing.
* Fear has crippled marriages and ministries.
* Fear has made people lose miracles, money and good initiatives lose momentum.

Fear can be conquered though; by actively putting your trust and confidence in God you begin your conquest of fear.

By a decision to resist it steadfastly. Fear can be conquered as you choose to praise God and walk in love. Fear can be conquered in your life by using the weapon God gave to you. Bring the blood against that spirit.

And they overcame him by the blood of the Lamb, and by the word of their testimony; and they loved not their lives unto the death.
Revelation 12:11 (KJV)

Apply the Word of God as your defence against fear. Nothing can withstand the two-edged sword of God's Word.

For the word of God is quick, and powerful, and sharper than any two edged sword, piercing even to the dividing asunder of soul and spirit, and of the joints and marrow, and is a discerner of the thoughts and intents of the heart.
Hebrews 4:12 (KJV)

Lastly raise the name of Jesus against every situation you face. We have been assured that whatever we ask in that name, we will not be put to shame.

So my friend it is time to lift your head and strengthen your arms. It is time to reach forth and take responsibility.

Take advantage of what the Lord has provided for you. Take your financial blessing; take your ministry back, everything the spirit of fear has stolen, every property under satan's covering and keep.

You now have the warrant of arrest with which you can subject and subdue the spirit of fear. Instead of you being the one to bow, it is time for you to realise you have been called, ordained and set up as an overcomer.

Look fear in the face and say I will not bow to adversity; I am a joint heir with God. Take the power by faith, take your destiny by faith and no matter what may rise against you, be able to say with a strong and bold heart, this too shall pass.

It is with such confidence that you are able to defeat satan, that you are able to take your place and reign in life instead of being made to bow at the face of every adversity.